UNCOVERING THE PAST:
ANALYZING PRIMARY SOURCES

WORKERS' RIGHTS

LYNN LESLIE PEPPAS

Crabtree Publishing Company
www.crabtreebooks.com

Author: Lynn Leslie Peppas
Editor-in-Chief: Lionel Bender
Editor: Simon Adams
Proofreader: Laura Booth,
  Wendy Scavuzzo, Anastasia Suen
Project coordinator: Petrice Custance
Design and photo research: Ben White
Production: Kim Richardson
**Production coordinator and
  prepress technician:** Ken Wright
Print coordinator: Margaret Amy Salter
Consultant: Amie Wright,
  The New York Public Library

Cover photo: THE HAYMARKET RIOT,
  1886. Wood engraving from contemporary
  American newspaper of the Haymarket
  Riot, Chicago, 1886.

Title page photo: Women worker finishing
  airplane parts at Consolidated Aircraft
  Corporation in Texas, 1942.

Photographs and reproductions:
Cover: The Granger Collection: Sarin Images
Getty Images: 34–35 (Bettmann), 37 (David McNew), 40–41 (STR/Stringer);
Library of Congress 3 (LC–USZ62–49516), 4, 6 Top Left (Icon) (LC–DIG–NCLC–
01339), 7 Btm (LC–DIG–ppmsca–28281), 8, 10, 12 Top Left (Icon) (hhh.ma1289/
color.570930c), 10–11 (LC–DIG–nclc–01455, 14, 16 Top Left (Icon) (LC–DIG–
ppmsca–26412), 16–17 (LC–DIG–ppmsca–26412), 24 (LC–DIG–ppmsca–38993)
31 (DIG–ds–05452), 32, 34, 36 Top Left (Icon) (LC–USE6–D–004357);
Shutterstock.com: 1, 27 (Everett Historical), 18, 20, 22, 24, 26, 28, 30 Top Left
(Icon), 38, 40 Top Left (Icon) (Hong Vo); Topfoto 4–5, 8–9, 9, 11, 12, 13 Top, 13
Btm, 14–15, 17, 18–19, 20, 20–21 22–23 Btm, 23, 25, 26, 28–29, 29 , 30–31, 36,
41 (The Granger Collection); 6–7 (SIPLEY/ClassicStock), 21 (World History
Archive), 32–33, 35 (The Image Works), 38–39 (The Image Works)
Map: Stefan Chabluk

This book was produced for
**Crabtree Publishing Company by
Bender Richardson White**

Library and Archives Canada Cataloguing in Publication

Peppas, Lynn, author
        Workers' rights / Lynn Peppas.

(Uncovering the past : analyzing primary sources)
Includes bibliographical references and index.
Issued in print and electronic formats.
ISBN 978-0-7787-2861-0 (hardback).--
ISBN 978-0-7787-2863-4 (paperback).--
ISBN 978-1-4271-1842-4 (html)

     1. Employee rights--Juvenile literature. 2. Labor laws and
legislation--Juvenile literature. 3. Industrial laws and legislation-
-Juvenile literature. I. Title.

HD6971.8.P47 2016   j331.01'1   C2016-903381-3
                                          C2016-903382-1

Library of Congress Cataloging-in-Publication Data

CIP available at the Library of Congress

Crabtree Publishing Company
www.crabtreebooks.com   1-800-387-7650

Printed in Canada/072016/PB20160525

Published in Canada
Crabtree Publishing
616 Welland Ave.
St. Catharines, ON
L2M 5V6

Published in the United States
Crabtree Publishing
PMB 59051
350 Fifth Avenue, 59th Floor
New York, NY 10118

Published in the United Kingdom
Crabtree Publishing
Maritime House
Basin Road North, Hove
BN41 1WR

Published in Australia
Crabtree Publishing
3 Charles Street
Coburg North
VIC, 3058

UNCOVERING THE PAST

INTRODUCTION: THE PAST COMES ALIVE 4
The importance of history and how it has shaped our lives today; an introduction to the labor movement.

HISTORICAL SOURCES: TYPES OF EVIDENCE 8
The use of primary and secondary sources; which one is the more reliable.

ANALYZING EVIDENCE: INTERPRETATION 14
Sourcing evidence, determining context, and revealing bias.

THE STORY UNCOVERED: WORKERS' RIGHTS 18
The struggle to achieve workers' rights, from the early 1800s to the 1960s; strike breaking, the legalization of trade unions, and limits on the working day.

EVIDENCE REVISITED: DIFFERENT VIEWS 32
The problems faced by immigrant and migrant workers and their struggles for their rights.

MODERN EXAMPLES: RECENT STRUGGLES 38
The continuing struggle for workers' rights in an international economic environment.

Timeline 42
Bibliography 44
Internet Guidelines..45
Glossary 46
Index 48

THE PAST COMES ALIVE

"What does labor want? . . . We want more schoolhouses and less jails; . . . more leisure and less greed; more justice and less revenge; in fact, more of the opportunities to cultivate our better natures . . . "

Samuel Gompers, American Federation of Labor leader, 1893

The past is everything that has ever happened up to this moment in time. **History** is the record of those events. Historians—people who study what has happened in the past—create histories by looking at something that has been saved or preserved from a particular time and place. These preserved records are called **primary sources**. They give historians a small window into what might have happened then.

Historians create their own **interpretations** of a historical time or event by closely investigating its primary sources. They ask questions about, or **analyze**, primary source materials and try to figure out what might have happened. But not every minute of an event can be preserved.

In this book, you are the historian who is studying the labor movement in North America. To do this, you must closely analyze **evidence** from primary sources from the past that have to do with employment and workers' rights. It is important to remember the past so we don't repeat the same mistakes.

The history of workers' rights and the labor movement was sometimes very violent. People suffered physically, mentally, and economically. But those individuals in the past fought hard to change workers' rights so that they, and future generations, would not continue to suffer. If we forget about sacrifices made in the past we might face the same problems and struggles in the future. Remembering what has and has not worked in the past will help make life easier for us today.

▲ This scene is only one part of a larger mural called *The Detroit Industry Murals* painted by Diego Rivera between 1923 and 1933. It depicts automobile industry workers on an assembly line.

The president of the Ford Motor Company, Edsel Ford, helped pay the artist to paint *The Detroit Industry Murals.* Would this fact change how the artist might have painted the workers? Can you tell which people are working? Why is there a group of people who are standing and watching the workers? Who might they be?

DEFINITIONS

We can define historical time in different ways:

A decade is a period of 10 years, a century is 100 years, and a millennium is 1,000 years.

Generation: Refers to a group of people who were born about the same time.

Era: A period of time dominated by an important characteristic, event, or person.

Age: A long period of time dominated by an important event, such as the Ice Age.

THE LABOR MOVEMENT

Civilizations from ancient times were almost entirely built by human labor. An organized workforce was necessary to provide food, shelter, and almost everything humans needed to sustain their way of life. Before the late 1700s, laborers were often builders, farmers, or **slaves.** Tradespeople were skilled laborers who worked at a specialized trade where they produced products, such as **textiles**, furniture, or weapons, entirely by hand.

The **Industrial Revolution** completely changed the way people lived and worked. It began in Great Britain in the late 1700s when the process of production shifted from hand-made to machine-made goods. In 1811, a group of textile workers in Great Britain called Luddites organized an action force because they were losing their jobs and being replaced by machines. The Luddites burned mills, destroyed industrial machines, attacked factory owners, and fought with British soldiers. The British government passed laws to stop the destruction of machinery by making the act a criminal offense punishable by execution.

The Industrial Revolution followed later in North America in about the mid-1800s. This shift from farming to industry is called **industrialization**. In industrial jobs, thousands of unskilled laborers worked in factories, repeating the same simple task over and over again.

Industrialization meant that industry owners—also called **capitalists**—controlled working conditions and wages. Before the 1900s, there were no laws that determined a minimum wage, maximum workweek, or proper working conditions for laborers. Capitalists

▲ This image of a slave market auction held in New Orleans in 1831 was hand-colored on an antique glass lantern slide sometime in the 1830s.

"The [members of the working class] have nothing to lose but their chains. They have a world to win. Working men of all countries, unite!"

From *The Communist Manifesto* by Karl Marx and Friedrich Engels, 1848

▶ This illustration, titled "The Slave-Market of To-Day", was created in 1884. It shows laborers being auctioned off to capitalists and manufacturers.

demanded that laborers work 12- to 18-hour days, six days a week, for unfair wages in unsafe working conditions. If a worker felt it was unfair, the owner would hire another laborer to take over their job because almost anyone could do the job. Something had to change for people to be able to support themselves and their families in a decent lifestyle. This was the beginning of the labor movement and the struggle for workers' rights.

ANALYZE THIS

How are these two images—the top painted in about 1830 and the bottom printed in about 1880—the same? What are the differences between the two people being auctioned for sale? What types of comparisons do you think the artist who painted the bottom painting wanted the viewer to make between slavery and laborers in the 1880s? Do you think these are fair comparisons? Why or why not?

TYPES OF EVIDENCE

"I wonder how they'd like to work as hard as we do, digging and drudging day after day, from morning till night, and then, every two or three years, have their wages reduced."

"A Second Peep at Factory Life" by Josephine L. Baker, Lowell, Massachusetts, from the *Lowell Offering*, 1845

A primary source is a piece of historical evidence that was created or witnessed during an era or event in the past. Primary sources are the most reliable sources of historical information and offer the best clues as to what really happened.

Primary sources can be:
- Photographs taken at the time or place of the event
- An interview with someone who experienced the event
- A map from the time or event you're researching
- Newspaper or magazine articles from the time of the event
- Documents, letters, or diary entries created at the time
- Physical objects, or artifacts, from the period of time

To find out if something is a primary source ask yourself this question: Was the person who created the primary source actually present during that time period or event? If the answer is yes, then it is a primary source.

You create primary sources every day. A shopping list, your homework assignment, your emails, texts, tweets, and Facebook posts could serve as historical evidence in the future. Imagine what a historian from the future could learn about people your age during this era by looking at the primary sources you've created just today!

▲ American artist Winslow Homer published his colored engraving, entitled "Factory: Bell Time", in *Harper's Weekly* in 1868. The image shows textile workers (men, women, and children) coming out of the factory.

LOWELL OFFERING

December, 1845.

"In God we a-e among the prophets."

A REPOSITORY
OF ORIGINAL ARTICLES, WRITTEN BY
"FACTORY GIRLS."

LOWELL: MISSES CURTIS & FARLEY.
BOSTON: JORDAN & WILEY, 121
Washington street.
1845.

◀ *Lowell Offering* was a monthly magazine that published stories and poems written by female textile workers in Lowell, Massachusetts, from 1840 to 1845.

SECONDARY SOURCES

A **secondary source** is one person's interpretation of what happened during a period of time or an event. The person creating it did not participate in, or witness, the historical event themself. Writers, historians, artists, and educators often investigate secondary sources to help them learn what happened.

Ask yourself the same question as before: Was the person creating this source of historical information actually present at that time? If the answer is no, the information is a secondary source. Secondary sources have used one or more primary sources to form opinions or reach conclusions. They have collected evidence and interpreted it for you already.

Secondary sources include:

- Encyclopedias
- Newspapers reporting on daily events in a certain area
- Textbooks
- Newspaper or magazine articles about an event in the past
- Maps created today to show historical information
- Interviews by an expert who did not directly experience a topic or an event

Secondary sources are a useful and entertaining way to learn about an event or period of time. Books, movies, documentaries, and television shows are all secondary sources. Primary sources often make you feel more emotionally connected to the event than a secondary source. For example, if I tell you that young children worked long hours in factories in

PERSPECTIVES

American photographer Lewis Hine published photographs of young children at work for the National Child Labor Committee between 1908 and 1924. He wanted his photos to prove that child laborers were being **exploited** in industrial jobs. What view do you form from looking at this photo of a child at work?

*"There were men who worked in the cooking-rooms, in the midst of steam and sickening odors, by artificial light; in these rooms the germs of **tuberculosis** might live for two years, but the supply was renewed every hour."*

From *The Jungle* by Upton Sinclair, 1906

the 1900s—this would be a secondary source because I wasn't actually there—you may be interested but have no emotional connection to the information. But when you investigate a primary source, such as this photograph by Lewis Hine showing a small child named Sadie Pfeifer working in a factory, you feel a stronger sense that this really did happen.

◀ **This young girl named Sadie Pfeifer had already been working for six months at the Lancaster Cotton Mills in Lancaster, South Carolina, when this photo was taken in 1908.**

Time Table of the Holyoke Mills,

To take effect on and after Jan. 3d, 1853.

The standard being that of the Western Rail Road, which is the Meridian time at Cambridge.

MORNING BELLS.

First Bell ring at 4.40, A. M.   Second Bell ring in at 5, A. M.

YARD GATES

Will be opened at ringing of Morning Bells, of Meal Bells, and of Evening Bells, and kept open ten minutes.

WORK COMMENCES

At ten minutes after last Morning Bell, and ten minutes after Bell which "rings in" from Meals.

BREAKFAST BELLS.

October 1st, to March 31st, inclusive, ring out at 7, A. M. ; ring in at 7.30, A. M.
April 1st, to Sept. 30th, inclusive, ring out at 6.30, A. M.; ring in at 7, A. M.

DINNER BELLS.

Ring out at 12.30, P. M. ; ring in at 1, P. M.

EVENING BELLS.

Ring out at 6.30,* P. M.

* Excepting on Saturdays when the Sun sets previous to 6.30.   At such times, ring out at Sunset.

In all cases, the *first stroke of the Bell* is considered as marking the time.

ANALYZE THIS

By studying this timetable, can you tell what time workers were expected to begin their workday? How many meals did they eat while at their job? How long was each meal break? How many hours were they expected to work? Is this a primary or a secondary source? How do you know?

◀ **This 1853 work schedule for textile workers from Holyoke Mills, Massachusetts, lists the hours workers were expected to work.**

FINDING RELIABLE SOURCES

Primary sources that are created closest to an event are the most reliable. For example, if a person present at an event was interviewed during the event, the record of their memory would be considered a more reliable source than if the same person was interviewed about the same event 20 years later.

Sometimes a primary source might give incorrect evidence. The best way to prove if a source is correct or not is to find another source that supports the same evidence. For example, if a diary entry reads that only women attended a meeting, a photograph of the same meeting showing only women might prove the evidence as fact. But if you find two primary sources about the same event that do not agree—for example, if the diary entry says a few men attended the meeting but a photo shows only women—then the information in one (or both) of the sources may be incorrect. You will have to dig further for more evidence!

The same rule applies to secondary sources as does primary sources. Secondary sources created closer to an event or era are considered more reliable than sources created later.

▼ A strike poster instructs Model Blouse Company employees in Millville, New Jersey, not to go into work because of a strike.

> Don't Go In! ▶ STOP!
> # Strike Today!
>
> Model Blouse Employees are ON STRIKE to end firing of UNION members, for JUST hours, FAIR wages, and DECENT working conditions!
>
> ***
>
> ALL OUT ON THE PICKET LINE FOR A COMPLETE
> ## UNION VICTORY
>
> Amalgamated Clothing Workers of America
> 19 E. Pine Street, Millville, N. J.
> license no. 24

ANALYZE THIS

This strike poster was printed in 1935. Who is the audience for this poster? Who created the poster? Why do they want workers to strike? What type of evidence does this poster tell you about the Model Blouse Company?

"We want a better America, an America that will give its citizens, first of all, a higher and higher standard of living so that no child will cry for food in the midst of plenty."

Sidney Hillman, American labor leader

◀ This is a membership certificate from the United Mine Workers of America from 1899.

▼ German-American artist Robert Koehler painted *The Strike* in 1886. The differences between the factory owners and their workers are clearly expressed.

INTERPRETATION

"The Labor Movement was the principal force that transformed misery and despair into hope and progress."

Dr. Martin Luther King, Jr., October 7, 1965

All primary sources were created for a specific reason. To analyze or understand a primary source, you must figure out what type of source it is, and who was meant to see or use it. This process is called **sourcing**. It involves asking yourself basic questions about the material you're looking at, such as these listed below:

- What is the source?
- Why was it created?
- When was it created?
- What else was happening around the same time?
- Can you find other primary sources that support or oppose the same ideas?

Sourcing helps you determine the **context**—the time and place—that a primary source relates to. In 1937, autoworkers in Flint, Michigan, held a sit-down strike against General Motors. The sit-down strike was first used in the United States in the early 1900s. Striking workers remained at their job stations so that employees couldn't hire other workers, known as strikebreakers, to come in and do the striking workers' jobs. This action stopped protests, that sometime turned violent, when strikebreakers replaced the workers. Sourcing a primary source, such as the photograph on this page, helps you more fully understand the evidence before you.

▶ **Strikers occupy the General Motors Fisher body plant #3 in Flint, Michigan, during the Flint Sit-down Strike in 1937.**

BIAS

Some sources target a large number of people while others might be for very few to see. For example, a photograph published in a magazine is for the public to view. The photographer may have been influenced to record an event in a particular way by the owner of the magazine. It may be reliable, but there is also a chance that it may be **biased** or presented in such a way as to persuade the viewer. But a diary entry is a personal source where the creator may believe that only he or she will ever read it. Most diarists do not have to worry about an audience and will therefore give a more truthful account. When analyzing a source, determining why and who a source was created for helps you better understand the evidence.

Sourcing helps to discover the bias a primary or secondary source of information was created with. Bias is the outlook, or opinions, that a person believes in. Everybody is biased to some degree by their educators, their caregivers, and their friends. The media, such as books, music, television, and the Internet, influences us, too. Anyone who creates primary or secondary sources can't help but be influenced by their personal bias. Just because a source has a bias does not mean it's bad or wrong. But it's up to you to decide how bias affects the meaning of the source you are analyzing.

▶ The capitalist business owner in Pittsburg is bathing in the light of "special **privilege**" and is well fed, well dressed, and is obviously enjoying himself. Meanwhile, on the other side, a large number of workers labor to hold the businessman up, in darkness.

"What good is industry if it be so unskillfully managed as not to return a living to everyone concerned? No question is more important than that of wages—most of the people in this country live on wages."

From *My Life and Work*, Henry Ford's autobiography, 1922

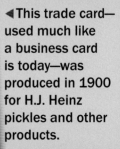

◄This trade card—
used much like
a business card
is today—was
produced in 1900
for H.J. Heinz
pickles and other
products.

WORKERS' RIGHTS

"Let our cry be REFORM – down with a moneyed aristocracy and up with the people."

William Sylvis, president of the National Labor Union, 1872

In the mid-1800s, millions of **immigrants** from Europe and Asia moved to North America in search of work. Slavery had existed in North America, but was **abolished** in Canada in 1834 and in the United States in 1865. This led to millions of newly **emancipated** African Americans joining the workforce. Because so many laborers were competing for jobs, black people were often discriminated against. Even though slavery was banned, African Americans were still treated unfairly in most workplaces.

The Industrial Revolution changed how North Americans lived and worked. Laborers worked in machine-operated factories instead of on a farm or in a specialized trade where a product, such as cloth, was produced by hand. This shift from farming to industry is a process called industrialization and it meant that industry owners controlled working conditions and wages.

Since there were a lot of laborers to choose from, industry owners made their employees work long hours in unsafe conditions for little pay. If someone complained, they would just hire another worker. Many people were angry with this type of treatment, so they joined together and decided to fight for change. This began the labor movement in North America.

In 1869, the most important American labor organization was established. This organization, known as the Knights of Labor, became a strong voice for workers' rights. All people were welcome to join the Knights, including skilled and unskilled laborers, women, immigrants, and African-American workers. The Knights of Labor soon spread internationally.

▼ This political cartoon, published in 1886, is entitled "The **Gospel** of the Knights of Labor." The artist, Joseph Keppler, emigrated from Austria to America around 1868.

ANALYZE THIS

In this image, "T.V. Powderly," the president of the Knights of Labor, is shown in the middle. The "scab," which is another name for strikebreaker, is on the left, and the "employer" which represents the capitalists, is on the right. Look at the positions of these characters. What do you think the artist was trying to show with this cartoon?

THE GILDED AGE

The Gilded Age, from the 1870s to 1890s, was an era when industry grew rich. Something "gilded" is gold-covered to make it look rich, but underneath it is not. During the Gilded Age a few capitalists or industry owners became very wealthy at the expense of millions of workers who suffered from poor working conditions and wages.

In 1872, the Nine-Hour Movement began in Hamilton, Ontario. Its goal was to **standardize** a nine-hour workday. Across central Canada workers joined Nine-Hour Leagues. When some faced criminal charges for creating a union and organizing a strike, Canada's prime minister John A. Macdonald introduced the Trade Unions Act. This act legalized **unions** in Canada. The Nine-Hour League strikers who had been charged were freed because it was no longer illegal to belong to a union. The Nine-Hour Movement did not succeed in reducing hours, but it did result in the legalization of trade unions and the formation of the Canadian Labor Union in May 1872.

In the United States, the Knights of Labor helped organize a general strike for an eight-hour workday in Chicago, Illinois, that began on May 1, 1886. On May 3, police officers killed two or more strikers during a violent outbreak at the McCormick plant. The next day, violence broke out again at a labor rally in Haymarket Square. Eight people were killed, including a police officer. Chicago police arrested hundreds of labor organizers afterward. Four of those arrested were found guilty, sentenced to the death penalty, and hanged for their role in the protest.

▲ "The Modern Colossus of [Rail] Roads," published during the Gilded Age in 1879, shows William Henry Vanderbilt, the most powerful person in the U.S. railroad industry. On his legs are two other powerful railroad industry figures— Cyrus West Field and Jay Gould.

"If there was no evidence to show that I was legally responsible [for setting off a bomb] then my conviction and the execution of the sentence is nothing less than willful, malicious, and deliberate murder. . . . For [the jury] themselves have fabricated most of the testimony which was used as a pretense to convict us . . . "

August Spies, labor organizer given the death sentence for his role in the Haymarket riot, October 1886

▶ During the late 1800s, many laborers in Chicago were German immigrants. This **handbill** written in both English and German tells Chicago laborers about the meeting in Haymarket Square.

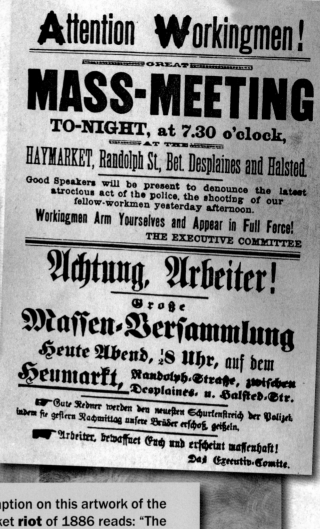

Attention Workingmen!

GREAT

MASS-MEETING

TO-NIGHT, at 7.30 o'clock,

AT THE

HAYMARKET, Randolph St., Bet. Desplaines and Halsted.

Good Speakers will be present to denounce the latest atrocious act of the police, the shooting of our fellow-workmen yesterday afternoon.

Workingmen Arm Yourselves and Appear in Full Force!

THE EXECUTIVE COMMITTEE

Achtung, Arbeiter!

Große

Massen-Versammlung

Heute Abend, ½8 Uhr, auf dem

Heumarkt, Randolph-Straße, zwischen Desplaines- u. Halsted-Str.

☞ Gute Redner werden den neuesten Schurkenstreich der Polizei, indem sie gestern Nachmittag unsere Brüder erschoß, geißeln,

☞ Arbeiter, bewaffnet Euch und erscheint massenhaft!

Das Executiv-Comité.

▼ The caption on this artwork of the Haymarket **riot** of 1886 reads: "The Anarchist Riot in Chicago—A dynamite bomb explodes among the police."

THE GILDED AGE ENDS

After the events of the Haymarket riot, the Knights of Labor membership declined greatly. Many turned instead to a labor organization that formed in December 1886 called the American Federation of Labor (AFL). The AFL was like the Knights in that it united existing unions but was not as **inclusive** as the Knights. It was led by Samuel Gompers.

Canadian workers organized the Trades and Labor Congress (TLC) in 1886. In 1889, the TLC created its Platform of Principles, which laid out the goals of the labor organization that included an eight-hour workday.

In 1892, a steel-mill owner in Homestead, Pennsylvania, decided to rid his plant of unionized workers. He cut their pay but the steelworkers refused to accept the pay cuts and the owner closed the mill. He then hired strikebreakers to replace the striking workers. Everybody in the town of Homestead was angry and many joined the strikers. A violent clash between agents trying to open the plant and strikers occurred on July 6, 1892, and resulted in ten deaths. State militia troops arrived to stop the violence. They allowed nonunion workers to operate the plant. In November unionized workers gave up the strike and came back to work as nonunionized labor.

▼ In 1894, U.S. president Grover Cleveland sent federal troops to Chicago to end the railroad workers strike, known as the Pullman Strike. Troops and strikers clashed and 600 train cars were set on fire. Union officials, including ARU president, Eugene Debs, were arrested, and workers returned to work as though nothing had happened.

"I found that the men were working for the Pullman company at wages upon which they could not live. I found that salaries had been cut time and again, until skilled mechanics were working their lives away for wages not sufficient for a day laborer."

Eugene Debs, American Railway Union (ARU) president, August 21, 1894

▲ The Knights of Labor held the first Labor Day parade in Union Square, New York City, on September 5, 1882.

EVIDENCE RECORD CARD

A painting of rioters during the Pullman strike
LEVEL Primary source
MATERIAL Newspaper illustration
LOCATION Chicago
DATE c.1894
SOURCE The Granger Collection/Topfoto

THE PROGRESSIVE MOVEMENT

By 1900, the push for reforms to workers' rights in North America gained more momentum. In 1901, Eugene Debs (former ARU president) founded the Socialist Party of America (SP). **Socialism** is the idea that production and distribution of goods (mines, mills, railways, etc.) should be owned and controlled by the country's government and not capitalists. The Industrial Workers of the World (IWW), sometimes called the "Wobblies," formed in 1905 with Bill Hayward as their leader.

Canada's federal government passed the Canada Labour Code Act in 1900. The act helped greatly to settle labor disagreements and promote fair wages and proper working conditions. Canadian laborers saw the success that labor organizations, such as the AFL and IWW, were achieving in the United States. They liked the experience and strength of the larger American-based unions. The TLC joined with the AFL in 1902. In fact, most

▼ Breaker boys were male children laborers between the ages of 8 and 12 who worked to break up larger pieces of coal into smaller pieces in coal mines.

ANALYZE THIS

This photograph of breaker boys at work in a Pennsylvanian mine was taken by Frances Benjamin Johnston in 1891. How old do you estimate these children are? The photographer was one of the first professional woman photographers in the United States. Why do you think she took this photograph? Do you think the boys know the photograph was being taken? Why or why not?

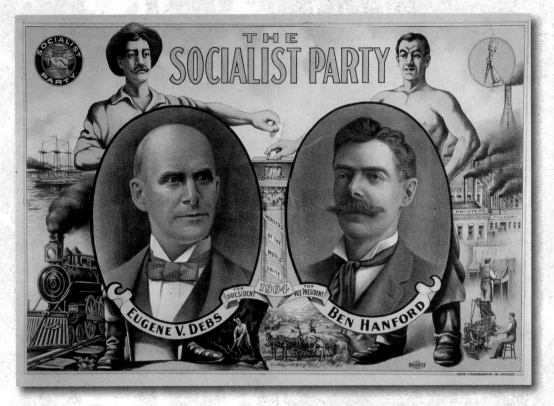

unions in Canada were American-based.

In the 1800s, children, often under 10-years-old, worked alongside their parents in factories and mines instead of going to school. In 1903, union organizer Mother Jones (Mary Harris Jones) led a protest march of striking child-laborers from Philadelphia to New York City to talk with President Roosevelt about the unfair working conditions for child laborers. The president refused to speak with them, but the march gained the support of many Americans. The National Child Labor Committee (NCLC) was formed in 1904 to investigate unfair working conditions for child laborers.

▲ A campaign poster for the Socialist Party of America in 1904 shows Eugene V. Debs running for president of the United States with Ben Hanford as his running-mate.

"We want the President to hear the wail of the children who never have a chance to go to school but work from ten to twelve hours a day in the textile mills of Philadelphia ... "

Mother Jones, 1903

EVIDENCE RECORD CARD

1904 Socialist Party of America campaign poster

LEVEL Primary source
MATERIAL Poster paper and ink
PUBLICATION Campaign poster
DATE 1903
SOURCE The Granger Collection/Topfoto

LABOR STRUGGLES

The Labor movement continued to struggle for labor rights throughout the 1900s. The Ludlow Massacre, which occurred in Colorado on April 20, 1914, was one of the most violent strikes. National troops and mining company guards opened fire on a tent colony of striking coal miners and their families, later setting fire to the camp. The violence resulted in the deaths of 21 men, women, and children.

Canada joined **World War I** in August 1914. The United States followed in April 1917. The global conflict began a boom in North American industry for the production of wartime goods. But much of the labor force was off to war and immigrant labor from Europe declined. Women therefore replaced men in the workforce in both the United States and Canada, but were not paid the same wages as the men they had replaced.

Striking unions enjoyed more power than ever before because industries needed their labor force working to meet demands. In the United States, President Wilson established the

▼ Royal North-West Mounted Police are shown charging down a Winnipeg street during the general strike on June 10, 1919.

"You struck a match and in the blaze that started,

You pulled the triggers of your gatling guns,

I made a run for the children but the fire wall stopped me.

Thirteen children died from your guns."

Lyrics from "Ludlow Massacre" by American singer/songwriter Woody Guthrie, 1944

National War Labor Board (NWLB) in 1918 to help solve conflicts between unions and industry leaders so that production would not be interrupted by strikes.

Unions remained powerful until World War I ended in 1918. Millions of men returned to their jobs and immigration from Europe resumed. Women, many unhappily, were replaced in the workforce.

In Canada during and after the war, the cost of living had risen but wages had not. In Winnipeg in 1919, almost 30,000 metal workers went on strike after their employers refused to negotiate fairer wages with the Metal Trades Council. Canadian government officials ordered the workers to return to work and the police force were brought in to arrest or **deport** union leaders and control the situation. The strike ended on June 26 after police killed two people and injured many others. Arrested union leaders were sentenced to jail, even after a Manitoba judge determined that the strike was a protest against unfair wages.

▶ The Triangle factory fire tragedy—reported here in *The (New York) World* newspaper—resulted in 146 workers dying in Manhattan, New York City, on March 25, 1911, due to unsafe working conditions.

THE GREAT DEPRESSION

In the United States, the 1920s was a time of industrial prosperity. But by 1929, however, industries began to slow down production. In October 1929, the **stock market** crashed and many lost their savings. Businesses laid off workers while those still employed faced cuts in pay, longer hours, and worse working conditions. By 1933, more than 1 million Americans were homeless and one quarter of America's workforce were unemployed. This Great **Depression**, as it was known, affected most countries around the world from 1929 to 1939.

In 1933, U.S. president Franklin D. Roosevelt created a program called the New Deal to help Americans recover from the Great Depression. The Works Progress Administration (WPA) created more than 3 million jobs to build or improve public streets and buildings. The National Labor Relations Act—also called the Wagner Act—protected the rights of workers to join unions. The Fair Labor Standards Act, passed in 1938, established workers' standards that included maximum working hours, a minimum wage, and a minimum age for child labor.

Canadian industries did not prosper like the Americans. Their economy

▶ Unemployed men are shown lining up outside an unemployment office in Harlem, New York City, in 1931.

ANALYZE THIS

This photograph shows men lined up outside an unemployment office in New York City in 1931. Why do you think so many of these men have turned their faces away when the photograph was being shot? Who are the two men standing outside of the roped off area where the majority of men are waiting? Why do you think they are present at this location?

"Values have shrunken to fantastic levels; taxes have risen; our ability to pay has fallen; . . . the withered leaves of industrial enterprise lie on every side; farmers find no markets for their produce; the savings of many years in thousands of families are gone."

President Franklin D. Roosevelt's inaugural speech, March 1933

never fully recovered, unemployment rose, and union memberships decreased. In 1932, the Canadian government organized relief camps—sometimes called Royal Twenty Centers—to provide shelter, food, and a small income for single, homeless, unemployed men. The men were, in turn, expected to do work such as construction of roads. In April 1935, about 1,000 relief workers from British Columbia went on strike, demanding better living conditions and work programs. Striking leaders spoke with Canadian prime minister Richard Bennett, but failed to gain any improvements. They organized a **rally**. Police officers and the Royal Canadian Mounted Police moved to arrest hundreds of strikers and a riot broke out on July 1. A police officer was killed and many were injured.

◀ Unemployed workers march in opposition to unemployment and its consequences in Toronto in 1931.

THE POST-WAR WORLD

Canada entered **World War II** in 1939 and the United States followed in 1941. And just as they had during World War I, industries throughout North America prospered from a surge in wartime production. North American women replaced young males in the workforce but, once again, were not paid the same wages for the same work.

After the war ended in 1945, membership in unions declined because industries offered better hours, wages, and working conditions. But in 1947, the American Congress passed the Taft-Hartley Act, partly in response to industries, such as coal mining, which went on strike during World War II. The Taft–Hartley Act banned **boycotts**—the refusal to do business with an organization as a means of protest—and held unions responsible for strike-related damages. Federal employees were banned from striking and employers were allowed to hire non-unionized people.

In the 1960s, the civil rights and women's rights movements were organized to stand up for their rights for equal pay and working conditions. Civil Rights' leader Martin Luther King Jr., gave his famous "I've Been to the

▲ During World War II, women workers took over production in wartime industries. These three women are working on a B-17 bomber at the Douglas Aircraft plant in California.

". . . the (Memphis) press dealt only with the window-breaking. I read the articles. They very seldom got around to mentioning the fact that one thousand, three hundred sanitation workers are on strike, and that Memphis is not being fair to them . . ."

Dr. Martin Luther King, Jr., Memphis, Tennessee, April 3, 1968

Mountaintop" speech at a rally for striking sanitation workers in Memphis, Tennessee, who were working in unsafe conditions and were discriminated against in the workplace. On February 12, 1968, about 1,000 black sanitation workers went on strike after two workers were crushed and died on the job because black workers were only allowed shelter from bad weather in the back of garbage trucks.

▼ An official U.S. Army poster published in 1944 shows three women at work for the war effort as an office worker, welder, and factory worker.

U.S. ARMY
OFFICIAL POSTER

SOLDIERS *without guns*

PERSPECTIVES

What job do you think each woman represents? Considering the title—"Soldiers Without Guns"— what do you think the audience is supposed to think about women workers? How are these three women similar? Do you think only young women worked during World War II? Why or why not?

EVIDENCE REVISITED

"All my life, I have been driven by one dream, one goal, one vision: to overthrow a farm labor system in this nation that treats farm workers as if they were not important human beings."

Cesar Chavez, farm workers organizer, November 9, 1984

Most of the millions of immigrant and **migrant** laborers who came to the United States and Canada to work came from Europe or Asia, where they had very little and were willing to work for low wages. North American capitalists took advantage of this cheap supply of immigrant labor. Many North American laborers—most were either immigrants or from immigrant families themselves—blamed newly arrived immigrants for taking their jobs and lowering wages.

In 1882, the U.S. Congress passed the Chinese Exclusion Act. This act restricted people from China from coming to the United States to work, and prevented the Chinese already working in America from becoming United States citizens. Canada's Immigration Act was amended in 1919 to restrict immigration to Canada because unemployment had risen after World War I. The amendment allowed the government to prohibit immigration due to a person's nationality or race, especially those who Canada had recently fought against in the war.

Even though the U.S. and Canadian governments passed laws to protect most workers by the 1960s, farmworkers and **domestic laborers**—jobs typically filled by immigrant or migrant workers—were not protected by these laws. Child labor laws did not protect the children of immigrants. As a result, migrant and immigrant workers suffered poor pay, long hours, and unsafe and unsanitary working conditions.

▶ **National Farm Workers Association president, Cesar Chavez (in the front, wearing a dark sweater), marches with grape strikers in Delano, California, on January 3, 1966.**

First grape strike by NFWA
LEVEL Primary source
MATERIAL Photograph
LOCATION Delano, California
DATE January 3, 1966
SOURCE The Image Works/
Topfoto

PERSPECTIVES

Farm workers' union organizer Cesar Chavez holds a "Huelga" flag. "Huelga" is the Spanish word for "strike." By looking at the marchers' faces, how do they feel about their protest? What are the ages and genders of the protesters?

STRIKES AND PROTESTS

In 1962, farm labor organizers Cesar Chavez and Dolores Huertes founded the National Farm Workers Association (NFWA), which later changed its name to the United Farm Workers (UFW). This union fought for the rights of workers in agricultural jobs. In 1965, the Filipino-American grape workers went on strike for better wages and working conditions. UFW members joined their strike. Chavez demanded that the strike remain non-violent and organized a nationwide boycott of grapes. UFW leader Jessica Govea led the boycott in Canada. In 1968, Chavez protested by **fasting** for 25 days. The strike lasted five years, before grape-farm owners agreed to better pay and conditions for their workers.

The immigrants' rights movement is ongoing. Today, there are millions of undocumented immigrants or **aliens**—meaning they are not citizens of the United States—who live and work in the country. Employers who hire undocumented immigrants can exploit them because they are not protected by labor laws and are afraid of being deported. However, on May 1, 2006—otherwise known as International Workers' Day—the Great American Boycott was organized. Organized by immigration rights groups and labor unions, supporters were asked to not buy or sell goods and not go to work or school in protest on this day.

In opposition to U.S. immigration, the Minuteman Project was organized by Jim Gilchrist in 2004 to stop undocumented immigrants coming from Mexico and from getting **humanitarian** help. The group patrolled areas along the U.S.–Mexico border where undocumented immigrants enter the United States.

▼ In May 1959, a mass **picket** took place at Mt. Sinai Hospital in New York City in support of striking hospital workers, many of them were African-American and Puerto Rican women striking for better wages.

"Go figure why the USA is $18 TRILLION in debt after so many decades of encouraging the transfer of poor and unskilled masses from Mexico and Central America (and other countries, too) into the United States."

Post on Minuteman Project website by Minuteman founder Jim Gilchrist, 2015

▲ Strikers and protestors from Syracuse University in New York demanding equal pay for equal work in 1998.

PERSPECTIVES

Compare these two photographs of strike protests, one taken in 1959 and the other photographed almost 40 years later in 1998. What remains the same and what is different?

MIGRANT INSECURITY

Migrant workers who come to Canada with time-limited work permits sometimes face exploitation from their employers. Exploited migrants often work in low-wage jobs such as hospitality, agriculture, or construction. They are only allowed to work for the employer named on their work permit and, as a result, do not report unfair treatment for fear of losing their job and having to leave the country. Many live with their employer and are afraid of becoming homeless if they protest unfair conditions. They are also not allowed to educate or train for other jobs by law.

In 2012, the Metcalfe Foundation of Canada reported on employer abuses of migrant workers. It listed a number of changes that should be made to improve migrant workers' rights in Canada.

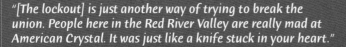

◀ In this cartoon published on April 4, 1891, entitled "Where the Blame Lies," American artist Grant Hamilton blamed anarchy, socialism, the Italian Mafia, and many other evils on unrestricted immigration.

ANALYZE THIS

What landmark has the artist illustrated that tells you this is Ellis Island in New York? Look closely at the expressions of the incoming immigrants. Do they look friendly? How do you think the artist wants you to think of them?

"[The lockout] is just another way of trying to break the union. People here in the Red River Valley are really mad at American Crystal. It was just like a knife stuck in your heart."

Paul Woinarowicz, American Crystal Sugar warehouse foreman, 2012

The Coalition for Migrant Workers Rights Canada was formed in 2015 and works to make the workplace safe and fair for all workers in Canada.

LOCKOUTS

A **lockout** is a tactic used by an owner of a business or industry in which they close and stop all work due to a labor disagreement. Owners do this to threaten unions and workers to accept their terms and conditions for labor. Sometimes during a strike, owners close industries altogether and relocate to another area or even country where labor is cheaper and laws are less restrictive. An example of a recent lockout occurred in 2012 at the American Crystal Sugar plant in Minnesota. Plant workers were locked out for almost two years before returning to work and accepting the offer originally made by the company.

ANALYZE THIS

This photograph was taken on May 1, 2007. How many different flags do you see? Notice the protest posters: What languages are they written in? What are some of the issues being protested? Notice the expressions of the protesters: How do you think they are feeling?

▲ The May Day demonstration in Los Angeles, California, on May 1, 2007, brought thousands of protestors parading through the streets on their way to a rally at City Hall.

RECENT STRUGGLES

"You know, today, women make up about half our workforce, but they still make 77 cents for every dollar a man earns. That is wrong, and in 2014, it's an embarrassment. Women deserve equal pay for equal work."

U.S. president Barack Obama, January 28, 2014

Industries in North America sometimes **outsource** their production to factories in other countries, mainly in Asia. They do this to exploit, or take advantage of, the low pay and minimal workers' rights in those countries. Yet unfair pay and poor working conditions still exist today in North America.

A **pay gap** is the difference of average pay between different groups of people, such as men and women or **Indigenous** women and women who are Caucasian or white. In the United States, depending on the individual state, women today still earn less money than men. In Canada in 2016, according to the Canadian Women's Foundation, Canadian women earn about 72 cents for every dollar earned by a man. The reasons for this are many. Women typically put in more hours of unpaid work (caring for children and household duties) than men. Women often work part time or at lesser paying jobs so they can juggle their domestic responsibilities.

In the United States in 2014, full-time female workers of African-American, Hispanic, Native American, or native Hawaiian ethnicities earned even less than white American women.

▶ Chinese immigrant women hold up protest signs in San Francisco, California, in front of an Apple store on June 17, 2010. The names on the protest signs are of Chinese workers at Foxconn factory in China who have committed suicide because of long hours and poor working conditions.

ANALYZE THIS

What can you read on these women's protest signs? What can you not read? Do you recognize the company and products they are standing in front of? Would this make you think twice about buying an Apple product? Why or why not?

Rao, Leqin. 18
饶丽清 18

Mr. Feng. 23
冯先生 23

C. Zhu. 2
祝昌明 2

FAIR TRADE

Fair trade is the purchase of goods for fair prices from workers or farmers worldwide. Fair trade organizations set a list of rules that ensure fair wages for workers. Consumers who believe in fair trade can buy products with a fair trade logo to know that the people who grew or produced the product were paid fairly for it!

THE FIGHT CONTINUES

In North America, strikes rarely happen today and are far less violent than historically. Today, North American workers often use a "work-to-rule" technique to protest a labor disagreement: They slow down and work as little as possible but still within their contract.

In 2016, the Alberta government in Canada passed the Enhanced Protection for Farm and Ranch Workers Act to protect paid workers on Alberta farms and ranches. The new law will set minimum hours, wages, and safety conditions to be met by employers in this industry.

Today, some North American workers are fighting to keep their jobs within their country. For example, in 2015 a cereal company laid off half its U.S. workers to relocate to Mexico. The Bakery, Confectionary, Tobacco Workers, and Grain Millers International Union (BCTGM) took the company to court in 2016. BCTGM believes the company is discriminating against minorities and employees more than 40 years of age, and violating the **collective bargaining** agreement.

Primary sources prove they have formed and joined unions, protested, boycotted, struck, and fought for the many changes that have occurred since the era of the 14-hour workday with no set minimum wage.

▲ Firefighters in Dhaka, Bangladesh, control a fire that broke out at this garment factory on November 26, 2012. U.S. and Canadian companies used the factory to make goods. No one was killed in this particular fire but more than 1,000 were killed in a similar collapse in the city.

"It is now my responsibility to support my three little brothers and sisters. I don't even want to live anymore. But I have to stay strong because of them. I have no one else besides them."

16-year-old Aruti Das, who lost her leg, and her mother, when a factory collapsed in Bangladesh

This photograph of a burned out garment factory in Bangladesh was taken in 2012. How does this image compare to images of American or Canadian firefighters responding to a factory fire? How do working conditions appear, and how easily do you think the workers were rescued?

MAY 2012 DAY

★ OCCUPY WALL STREET STANDS IN SOLIDARITY WITH THE CALLS FOR... ★

ON MAY DAY • WHEREVER YOU ARE • WHOEVER YOU ARE

NO WORK

NO SCHOOL

NO CHORES

NO SHOPPING

NO BANKING

A DAY WITHOUT THE 99% • A GENERAL STRIKE AND MORE!!

TAKE THE STREETS!

▶ The back cover of the March 2012 issue of *Tidal,* a political magazine that supported the Occupy **Wall Street** anti-capitalist protest. The "99%" are everyday consumers and workers who financially support the 1 percent of very wealthy capitalists.

TIMELINE

1800

1800s Industrial Revolution begins in North America

1834 Slavery is abolished in Canada

1865 Slavery is abolished in United States

1869 Knights of Labor founded in the United States

1870s–1890s Gilded Age in North America

1872 Trade Unions Act is passed in Canada; Canadian Labor Union founded

1882 Chinese Exclusion Act passed in United States

1886 Trades and Labor Congress founded in Canada; American Federation of Labor founded in United States

May 1, 1886 Eight-Hour Movement begins in Chicago

May 4, 1886 Haymarket Affair; Police officer and protesters killed during rally

July 6, 1892 Ten people die during strike at Homestead, Pennsylvania

1900

1900 Canadian government passes the Canada Labour Code

1901 Socialist Party of America is founded

April 20, 1914 Striking miners and their families are shot during the Ludlow Massacre

August 1914 Canada enters World War I

1917 United States enters World War I

June 21, 1919 Police officers open fire and kill two protesters on Bloody Saturday

June 26, 1919 Winnipeg General Strike ends

1929 Great Depression begins after U.S. stock market crashes

1932 Relief camps set up for unemployed and single Canadian males

1933 U.S. president Franklin D. Roosevelt creates New Deal

1938 Fair Labor Standards Act established; creates minimum wage, maximum working hours, and minimum age for child labor

April 1935 Canadian Relief Camp workers strike

1939

1939 Canada enters World War II

1941 United States enters World War II

1962 National Farm Workers Association (NFWA) is founded by Cesar Chavez and Dolores Huertes

May 1, 2006 International Workers Day; Great American Boycott is organized

2015 Coalition for Migrant Workers Rights, Canada, founded

1940

2016

1947 Taft-Hartley Act passed, banning federal employees from striking

1965 Filipino-American grape workers strike

2004 Minuteman Project founded by Jim Gilchrist

April 2015 Factory outsourcing clothing for North American market in Bangladesh collapses, killing more than 1,000 workers

Industrial areas of North America

BIBLIOGRAPHY

QUOTATIONS

p.4 Gompers, Samuel. "What Does Labor Want?" www.gompers.umd.edu/1893%20more%speech.html

p.6 Marx, Karl and Engels, Friedrich. The Communist Manifesto, 1948 and Karl Marx: *The Revolutions of 1848: Political Writings,* 1973.

p.8 Baker, Josephine L. *Lowell Offering.* www.albany.edu/history/history316/SecondPeepatFactoryLife.html

p.10 Sinclair, Upton. *The Jungle.* www.gutenberg.org/ebooks/140

p.12 Hillman, Sidney. www.dol.gov/general/aboutdol/hallofhonor/1992_hillman

p.14 King, Dr. Martin Luther Jr. www.americanrhetoric.com/speeches/mlkivebeentothemountaintop.html

p.16 Ford, Henry. *My Life and Work.* www.gutenberg.org/ebooks/7213

p.18 Sylvis, William. "The Life, Speeches, Labors and Essays of William H. Sylvis." https://archive.org/details/lifespeecheslab00sylvgoog

p.21 Spies, August. http://chicagohistory.org/hadc/books/b01/B01S001.html

p.22 Debs, Eugene. Article from *Omaha Daily Bee,* August 21, 1894. http://chroniclingamerica.loc.gov/lccn/sn99021999/1894-08-21/ed-1/seq-3/

p.25 Jones, Mary Harris. "March of the Mill Children" http://explorepahistory.com/odocument.php?docId=1-4-235

p.26 Guthrie, Woody. "Ludlow Massacre" lyrics: http://woodyguthrie.org/Lyrics/Ludlow_Massacre.html

p.28 Roosevelt, Franklin D. inaugural speech, March 1933. https://www.archives.gov/education/lessons/fdr-inaugural/

p.30 King, Dr. Martin Luther, Jr. www.americanrhetoric.com/speeches/mlkivebeentothemountaintop.html

p. 32 Cesar Chevez. https://libraries.ucsd.edu/farmworkermovement/essays/essays/CESAR%20CHAVEZ%20COMMONWEALTH%SPEECH.pdf

p.34 Gilchrist, Jim. Post of Minutemen Project website. http://baesic.net/minutemanproject/minuteman-project-leader-endorses-donald-trump-for-president-suggests-cruz-run-as-vp/

p.36 Woinarowicz, Paul. *The New York Times,* January 23, 2012. www.nytimes.com/2012/01/23/business/lockouts-once-rare-put-workers-on-the-defensive.html?_r=0

p.38 Obama, Barack. State of the Union address, January 28, 2014. https://www.whitehouse.gov/the-press-office/2014/01/28/president-barack-obamas-state-union-address

p.40 Das, Aruti. "Joe Fresh continuing garment business in Bangladesh in year after tragedy." www.cbc.ca/news/world/joe-fresh-continuing-garment-business-in-bangladesh-in-year-after-tragedy-1.2606120

TO FIND OUT MORE

Non-fiction:

Atkins, S. Beth. *Voices from the Fields: Children of Migrant Farmworkers Tell Their Stories.* New York, Little, Brown, 2000.

Burgan, Michael. *Breaker Boys: How a Photograph Helped End Child Labor.* Mankato, Minn., Capstone, 2012.

Lawrence, Katherine. *Labor Legislation: The Struggle to Gain Rights for American Workforce.* New York, Rosen, 2006.

McNeese, Tim. *The Labor Movement: Unionizing America.* New York, Chelsea House, 2008.

Marrin, Albert. *Flesh and Blood So Cheap: The Triangle Fire and Its Legacy.* New York, Knopf, 2011.

Fiction:

Greenwood, Barbara. *Factory Girl.* Toronto, Kids Can Press, 2007.

Haddix, Margaret Peterson. *Uprising.* New York, Simon and Schuster, 2011.

Markel, Michelle. *Brave Girl Clara and the Shirtwaist Makers' Strike of 1909.* New York, Balzer + Bray, 2014.

INTERNET GUIDELINES

Finding good source material on the Internet can sometimes be a challenge. When analyzing how reliable the information is, consider these points:

- Who is the author of the page? Are they an expert in the field or a person who experienced the event?
- Is the site well known and up-to-date? A page that has not been updated for several years probably has out-of-date information.
- Can you verify the facts with another site? Always double-check information.

- Have you checked all possible sites? Don't just look on the first page a search engine provides. Remember to try government sites and research papers.
- Have you recorded website addresses and names? Keep this data so you can backtrack and verify the information you want to use.

WEBSITES:

Library of Congress National Child Labor Committee Collections
View more than 5,000 photographs from the National Child Labor Committee taken between 1908 and 1924.
www.loc.gov/pictures/collection/nclc/

Library of Congress Newspaper and Current Periodical Reading Room
Read about the Haymarket Affair as reported by American newspapers during the era.
www.loc.gov/rr/news/topics/haymarket.html

Canadian Museum of History
Contains a history of labor movement in Canada with primary source materials.
www.historymuseum.ca

Digital History
Learn about the labor movement during the Gilded Age and Progressive Era in the United States. Website includes primary source materials.
www.digitalhistory.uh.edu

New York Public Library
A website with more than 100 photographs concerning labor, housing, and social conditions in the United States by photographer Lewis Hine.
http://digitalcollections.nypl.org/collections/photographs-concerning-labor-housing-and-social-conditions-in-the-united-states#/?tab=about

The Newberry Digital Collections for the Classroom
A wealth of information on American labor movements that include the Haymarket Affair, Pullmans, Garment Workers' strike, and more. Primary source documents enhance the learning experience.
http://dcc.newberry.org/collections/chicago-workers-during-the-long-gilded-age

GLOSSARY

abolish To put an end to

aliens People who are not citizens of the United States

analyze To study carefully

aristocracy A class of people who are born into a titled family

bias The outlook, perspective, or opinions, that a person believes in

boycott To stop using or refusing to buy something

capitalist A person who owns a business or company for personal gain

collective bargaining The process of negotiating wages, hours, and working conditions between a union and an employer

colossus A person or thing of extreme size and importance

context The setting, time, or place of a source. It includes the social customs and culture that shape the generation of people living through that era or period.

deport To return a person to their home country

depression A time of economic hardship

domestic laborer A person who cares for a home and children

emancipate To set a person free from another person's control

evidence The body of facts, clues, or information to show whether something is true

exploit To take unfair advantage of

fast To choose not to eat for a specific reason

gospel A guide or book of religious teachings

handbill An advertisement printed on paper and handed out to people

history Past events and their description

humanitarian A person who tries to help others

immigrant A person who has recently moved from his or her home country to another country

inclusive Open to everyone

Indigenous Produced, living, or existing naturally in a particular region or environment

Industrial Revolution The major change in production from hand-made to machine-made goods

industrialization A shift in labor from farming to industry

interpret To study further to understand something

lockout A tactic used by an owner of a business or industry in which they close and stop all work due to a labor disagreement

migrant A person who travels from one country to another to live and work

outsource To send work to be done by people outside of the company's home country

pay gap The difference in average pay between different groups of people

picket To protest by standing or marching while holding a sign that shows what a person is protesting against

primary source A firsthand memory, account, document, or artifact from the past that serves as a historical record about what happened at a particular time

privilege Special rights or advantages given to someone that not everyone enjoys

races Groups of people each with their own language, culture, and history

rally A meeting or gathering of people to support a cause

reform To make changes and improvements

riot A public disturbance by a large crown in protest against something

secondary source A historian's or artist's interpretation of a primary source

slave A person owned by another and treated as property without any rights; a slave is often forced to work for no pay and poor working conditions

socialism A political and economic theory that advocates that the means of production, distribution, and exchange should be owned or regulated by the community as a whole

sourcing To locate, identify, and analyze a source of evidence by working out what type of source it is, who was meant to see it, and for what purpose

standardize To set guidelines for all to follow

stock market A place where shares in a business are bought and sold

technique A plan or a particular way of dealing with a problem or issue

textile Cloth

tuberculosis A serious lung disease that is often fatal if not treated

union A group of workers who join together to work out labor issues with the owners of a company or business

Wall Street The major financial district in New York City, where the stock exchange and many banks are located

World War I War fought from 1914 to 1918 between the United States, Canada, the United Kingdom, France, Italy, Japan, and their allies against Germany, Austria-Hungary, the Ottoman Empire (Turkey), and their allies; the United States did not enter the war until 1917

World War II War fought from 1939 to 1945 between the United States, Canada, Britain, France, the U.S.S.R., and their allies against Nazi Germany, Italy, Japan, and their allies; the United States, the U.S.S.R, and Japan did not join the war until 1941

INDEX

African Americans
  18, 22, 31, 34, 38
American Federation of
  Labor 22, 24

Baker, Josephine L. 8
Bangladesh 40–41
bias 16

Canada Labour Code Act 24
capitalists 6–7, 16–17, 21
Chavez, Cesar 32–33, 34
child labor 10–11, 24, 25,
  32
Cleveland, Grover 22
Communist Manifesto, The
  6
context 14

Das, Aruti 40
Debs, Eugene 22, 23, 24,
  25
Depression, the Great
  28–29

Engels, Friedrich 6
evidence 4, 8, 10, 12

fair trade 40
Ford, Edsel 5
Ford, Henry 16
Ford Motor Company 5

General Motors 14
Gilchrist, Jim 34
Gilded Age, the 20–21
Gompers, Samuel 4, 22
Great American Boycott 34
Guthrie, Woody 26

Hamilton, Grant 36
Haymarket riot 20–21, 22
Hayward, Bill 24

Hine, Lewis 10–11
Holyoke Mills 11
Homer, Winslow 8
Homestead steelworkers
  22
Huertes, Dolores 34

immigrants 18, 26–27, 32,
  34, 36, 38
Industrial Revolution, the
  6, 18
industrialization 6, 18
International Workers of the
  World 24

Keppler, Joseph 18
King, Jr., Dr. Martin Luther
  14, 30
Knights of Labor, the
  18–19, 21, 22–23
Koehler, Robert 13

Labor Day parade 23
Lancaster Cotton Mills 11
lockouts 37
Lowell Offering 8–9
Luddites, the 6
Ludlow Massacre 26

Macdonald, John A. 20–21
Marx, Karl 6
Memphis sanitation workers
  31
Minuteman Project 34
Mouse Blouse Company 12

National Child Labor
  Committee 25
National Farm Workers
  Association 32–33, 34
National War Labor Board
  27
New Deal, the 28

Nine-Hour Movement, the
  20–21

Occupy Wall Street 41
outsourcing 38, 40

pay gap 38
Pfeifer, Sadie 10–11
primary sources 4, 8, 10–
  11, 12, 14, 16
Pullman strike 22–23

Rivera, Diego 4–5
Roosevelt, Franklin D. 28
Royal Twenty Centers 21

scabs 19, 22
secondary sources 10–11,
  12, 16
Sinclair, Upton 10
sit-down strike 15
slaves and slavery 6–7, 18
Socialist Party of America
  24, 25

Taft–Hartley Act 30
Trades and Labor Congress
  22, 24
Triangle factory fire 27

unemployment 28–29
United Mine Workers of
  America 13

Vanderbilt, William Henry
  21

Winnipeg strike 27
Woinarowicz, Paul 36
World War I 26–27, 32
World War II 30, 31